WHERE ARE THEY?

FIND FREDDIE

LOOK FOR LISA

HUNT FOR HECTOR

SEARCH FOR SAM

MORE THAN 1,000 FUN THINGS TO SEARCH AND FIND

FOUR BOOKS IN ONE

By

Anthony Tallarico

kidsbooks® Incorporated

FIND FREDDIE

WHERE ARE THEY?

FIND FREDDIE
AT HOME AND . . .

- ☐ Alligator
- ☐ Apple
- ☐ Big foot
- ☐ Bird's nest
- ☐ Boxing glove
- ☐ Bug
- ☐ Cupcake
- ☐ Deflated balloon
- ☐ Dinosaur
- ☐ 4 Drumsticks
- ☐ Eight ball
- ☐ Electric guitar
- ☐ False teeth
- ☐ Fire hydrant
- ☐ Football helmet
- ☐ Footprints
- ☐ Giant pencil
- ☐ "Goof Off" medal
- ☐ 2 Hamburgers
- ☐ Lifesaver
- ☐ 2 Locomotives
- ☐ Magnifying glass
- ☐ Mailbox
- ☐ Model plane
- ☐ Monster hand
- ☐ Mouse house
- ☐ 3 Music notes
- ☐ Paintbrush
- ☐ Ping-pong net
- ☐ "Quarantine"
- ☐ Sled
- ☐ Slice of pizza
- ☐ Snake
- ☐ Soccer ball
- ☐ 3 Speakers
- ☐ Tent
- ☐ Thermometer
- ☐ "Think Small"
- ☐ 13:15
- ☐ Top hat
- ☐ Toy car
- ☐ Tricycle
- ☐ "Yech!"
- ☐ Yo-yo

FIND FREDDIE
IN SPACE AND . . .

FIND FREDDIE AT THE BEACH AND . . .

- ☐ Angry dog
- ☐ Angry horse
- ☐ Bulldozer
- ☐ Caddy
- ☐ Castle
- ☐ 3 Cats
- ☐ Eskimo
- ☐ Firefighter
- ☐ 3 Football players
- ☐ Hungry fish
- ☐ Hungry lion
- ☐ 2 Ice cream cones
- ☐ Kangaroo
- ☐ Launch site
- ☐ Laundry
- ☐ Life raft
- ☐ Mailbox
- ☐ Motorcyclist
- ☐ "New Sand"
- ☐ Octopus
- ☐ Oil well
- ☐ Paint-by-number
- ☐ Panda
- ☐ Periscope
- ☐ Policeman
- ☐ "Quicksand"
- ☐ 2 Radios
- ☐ Record
- ☐ Robot
- ☐ Rock surfer
- ☐ Seahorse
- ☐ Sea serpent
- ☐ Seltzer bottle
- ☐ Singing cowboy
- ☐ Snail
- ☐ Strong wind
- ☐ 3 Tires
- ☐ Tuba player
- ☐ 6 Turtles
- ☐ Twin boys
- ☐ 8 Umbrellas
- ☐ "Used Sand"
- ☐ Very fat man
- ☐ Wet dog

FIND FREDDIE AT SCHOOL AND...

- ☐ Apple
- ☐ Awakening monster
- ☐ Balloon
- ☐ "Ban Homework"
- ☐ Bare feet
- ☐ 2 Baseball bats
- ☐ Baton twirler
- ☐ Bowling ball
- ☐ Boy Scout
- ☐ Cake
- ☐ Cannon
- ☐ Clock setter
- ☐ Coach
- ☐ Cook
- ☐ "Disco"
- ☐ Explosion
- ☐ Fish tank
- ☐ Guitar
- ☐ Headless horseman
- ☐ Helium filled bubble gum
- ☐ Jump rope
- ☐ Lost ear
- ☐ Mouse attack
- ☐ Pumpkin
- ☐ 2 Rabbits
- ☐ 5 Report cards
- ☐ Roller skates
- ☐ Robot
- ☐ Rocket launch
- ☐ "Room To Let"
- ☐ 4 "School Closed" signs
- ☐ Secret trap door
- ☐ Ship
- ☐ 2 Sleeping students
- ☐ Snake
- ☐ Soccer practice
- ☐ Surfboard
- ☐ Tent
- ☐ Tuba
- ☐ 4 TV antennae
- ☐ Tyrannosaurus
- ☐ Water bomb
- ☐ Weightlifter

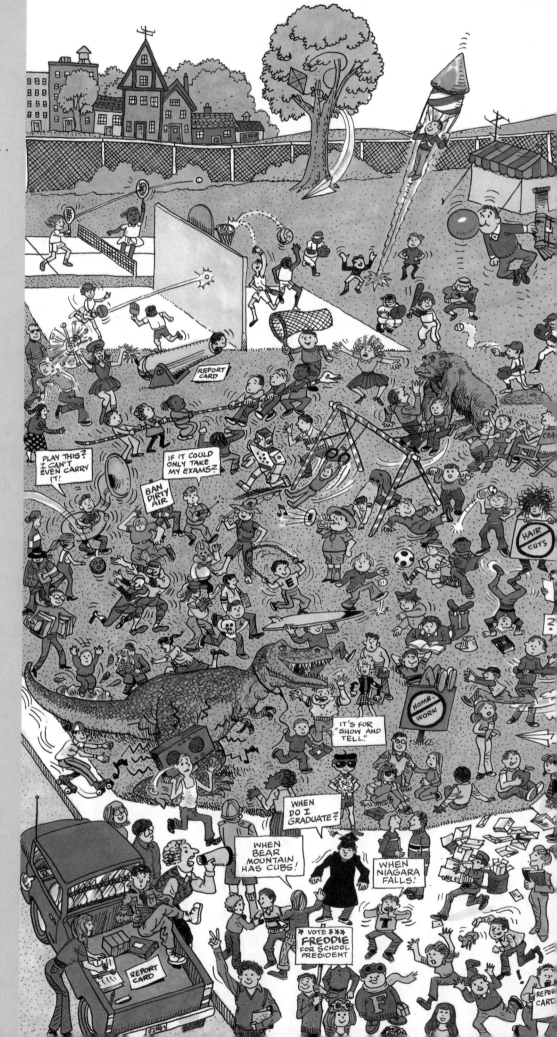

FIND FREDDIE
ON THE SCHOOL
BUS TRIP AND . . .

- [ ] Airplane
- [ ] Alligator
- [ ] Ambulance
- [ ] 5 Balloons
- [ ] Banana
- [ ] Barbershop
- [ ] Birdcage
- [ ] Boat
- [ ] "Bubble Gum Co."
- [ ] Burger-mobile
- [ ] Circus tent
- [ ] 3 Clocks
- [ ] Closed road
- [ ] Covered wagon
- [ ] Diver
- [ ] Doghouse
- [ ] Donkey
- [ ] Fish-mobile
- [ ] Garbage truck
- [ ] Gas station
- [ ] Ghost
- [ ] Horseshoe
- [ ] Hotel
- [ ] Igloo-mobile
- [ ] Jack-in-the-box
- [ ] Jellybean factory
- [ ] Lake serpent
- [ ] Library
- [ ] Locomotive
- [ ] 2 Mice
- [ ] Milk truck
- [ ] One-eyed monster
- [ ] Sailor cap
- [ ] Sandwich
- [ ] "72"
- [ ] 4 Sheep
- [ ] "Shopping Mall"
- [ ] 2 Skulls
- [ ] Sombrero
- [ ] Teepee-mobile
- [ ] Telephone
- [ ] Telescope
- [ ] Tennis racket
- [ ] Tow truck
- [ ] 2 Used tires

FIND FREDDIE AT THE MOVIES AND . . .

- ☐ Artist
- ☐ 2 Baby carriages
- ☐ Baby nerd
- ☐ 10 Balloons
- ☐ Barber pole
- ☐ Baseball game
- ☐ Birdcage
- ☐ 3 Cars
- ☐ Cook
- ☐ Count Dracula
- ☐ 3 Cries for "help"
- ☐ Detective
- ☐ 2 Dogs
- ☐ Duck
- ☐ Dunce cap
- ☐ Elephant
- ☐ Fisherman
- ☐ Football
- ☐ 2 Football players
- ☐ "For Sale"
- ☐ 3 Ghosts
- ☐ Giraffe
- ☐ 2 Gorillas
- ☐ "Hector"
- ☐ Ice cream cone
- ☐ Jogger
- ☐ 2 Keystone cops
- ☐ Man falling asleep
- ☐ Mouse
- ☐ 5 Paper airplanes
- ☐ Red wagon
- ☐ Sailboat
- ☐ "Seymour At The Movies"
- ☐ Scuba diver
- ☐ Skateboard
- ☐ Skier
- ☐ Snowman
- ☐ Tic-tac-toe
- ☐ Turtle
- ☐ 2 Ushers
- ☐ Volcano
- ☐ "Wet Paint"
- ☐ Witch

FIND FREDDIE
IN MONSTERVILLE
AND . . .

- ☐ 6 Arrows
- ☐ Bathbrush
- ☐ 13 Bats
- ☐ Ben Franklin
- ☐ Broken clock
- ☐ Broken heart
- ☐ Carrot
- ☐ Clothespin
- ☐ Cowgirl
- ☐ Daisy
- ☐ "Dead End"
- ☐ Dog
- ☐ Eye in the sky
- ☐ Flying carpet
- ☐ Garbage can
- ☐ 6 Ghosts
- ☐ "Harvard Drop-Out"
- ☐ Humpty Dumpty
- ☐ Ice cream cone
- ☐ Key
- ☐ "Kids Ahead"
- ☐ Kite
- ☐ Ladder
- ☐ Mailbox
- ☐ Mail carrier
- ☐ Ms. Transylvania
- ☐ "No Fishing"
- ☐ 3 Number 13's
- ☐ One-eyed monster
- ☐ "One way"
- ☐ Octopus
- ☐ 7 Pumpkins
- ☐ Rabbit
- ☐ Skeleton
- ☐ 8 Skulls
- ☐ Sprinkler
- ☐ Tic-tac-toe
- ☐ Truck
- ☐ TV set
- ☐ Weird doctor
- ☐ 2 Welcome mats
- ☐ Window washer
- ☐ Witch
- ☐ Young Dracula's wagon

FIND FREDDIE
AT THE AIRPORT
AND . . .

- ☐ Arrow
- ☐ Banana peel
- ☐ 3 Bats
- ☐ Bear
- ☐ Bird in love
- ☐ Boots
- ☐ Bride and groom
- ☐ Chicken
- ☐ Clown
- ☐ Cow
- ☐ Dart
- ☐ Dog pilot
- ☐ "Don't Fly"
- ☐ "Fly"
- ☐ Flying saucer
- ☐ 4 Fuel trucks
- ☐ Globe
- ☐ Golfer
- ☐ Hockey stick
- ☐ Horse
- ☐ "ICU2"
- ☐ Leaping lizard
- ☐ Long beard
- ☐ Luggage carrier
- ☐ "One Way"
- ☐ 3 Paper planes
- ☐ Photographer
- ☐ Pterosaur
- ☐ Rabbit
- ☐ 2 Sailboats
- ☐ Santa Claus
- ☐ Seesaw
- ☐ Sherlock Holmes
- ☐ Shooting star
- ☐ Space capsule
- ☐ "Star Wreck"
- ☐ Super hero
- ☐ Telescope
- ☐ Teepee
- ☐ 2 Unicorns
- ☐ Walnut
- ☐ Watermelon
  slice
- ☐ Windsock
- ☐ Winged man
- ☐ Wooden leg

FIND FREDDIE
AT THE BALLPARK
AND . . .

- [ ] Basketball
- [ ] 3 Beach balls
- [ ] 3 Birds
- [ ] Bone
- [ ] Boxing glove
- [ ] Bubble gum bubble
- [ ] Car
- [ ] Clothesline
- [ ] Cyclist
- [ ] 3 Dancers
- [ ] Elephant
- [ ] Fish
- [ ] Football team
- [ ] Frankenstein monster
- [ ] Ghost
- [ ] Giraffe
- [ ] Gorilla
- [ ] "Happy Section"
- [ ] 3 Hearts
- [ ] Horse
- [ ] 2 "Hot" dogs
- [ ] Lawn mower
- [ ] Lost shoe
- [ ] Mascot
- [ ] Monster hand
- [ ] 6 "No. 1" hands
- [ ] "Out" banner
- [ ] Painter
- [ ] 5 Paper airplanes
- [ ] Parachutist
- [ ] Rabbit
- [ ] Showers
- [ ] Sleeping player
- [ ] Snowman
- [ ] Tic-tac-toe
- [ ] Torn pants
- [ ] Turtle
- [ ] 4 TV cameras
- [ ] 2 TV sets
- [ ] Two-gloved fan
- [ ] 3 Umbrellas
- [ ] Uncle Sam
- [ ] Viking
- [ ] Yellow slicker

FIND FREDDIE
AT THE MUSEUM
AND . . .

FIND FREDDIE IN THE OLD WEST TOWN AND . . .

- ☐ Alien
- ☐ Bald Indian
- ☐ Banana peel
- ☐ Bearded man
- ☐ 7 Bedbugs
- ☐ Boot Hill
- ☐ 6 Cactuses
- ☐ Cat
- ☐ "Condos"
- ☐ 5 Ducklings
- ☐ Fire hydrant
- ☐ Fistfight
- ☐ Flying saucer
- ☐ "Ghost Town"
- ☐ Hand-in-a-box
- ☐ Hobo hitchhiker
- ☐ Jailbreak
- ☐ Jockey
- ☐ Lasso
- ☐ Long johns
- ☐ One-man-band
- ☐ Painted mountain
- ☐ Parking meter
- ☐ Piano player
- ☐ Piggy bank
- ☐ 3 Rabbits
- ☐ Rain cloud
- ☐ Rhinoceros
- ☐ Rocking horse
- ☐ Satellite dish
- ☐ Shark fin
- ☐ Sharpshooter
- ☐ Sheriff
- ☐ Snake
- ☐ Snowman
- ☐ Soccer ball
- ☐ Stampede
- ☐ "Tacos"
- ☐ 8 Teepees
- ☐ "Texas"
- ☐ Theater
- ☐ 2 Tombstones
- ☐ Unicorn
- ☐ Witch

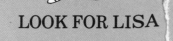

FIND FREDDIE   LOOK FOR LISA   HUNT FOR HECTOR   SEARCH FOR SA

HUNT FOR HECTOR
AT THE DOG HALL
OF FAME
AND . . .

- ☐ Alien
- ☐ Astronaut
- ☐ Automobile
- ☐ Babe Ruff
- ☐ 2 Birds
- ☐ Boot
- ☐ "Buffalo Bull"
- ☐ Cannon
- ☐ Cat
- ☐ "Cave Dog"
- ☐ Clown
- ☐ Cook
- ☐ Doghouse
- ☐ "Down Boy"
- ☐ Elephant
- ☐ Fallen star
- ☐ Flying dog
- ☐ Football
- ☐ Ghost dog
- ☐ 2 Giant bones
- ☐ Guard dog
- ☐ Hot dog
- ☐ Husky
- ☐ Indian
- ☐ Juggler
- ☐ Kangaroo
- ☐ Man on leash
- ☐ Mirror
- ☐ Moon
- ☐ Mouse
- ☐ Napoleon
- ☐ Photographer
- ☐ Pilgrim
- ☐ Pirate flag
- ☐ Record player
- ☐ Santa hound
- ☐ Sheep
- ☐ Sherlock Bones
- ☐ Stamp
- ☐ Super hero
- ☐ Super poodle
- ☐ Target
- ☐ Tin can
- ☐ Umpire

HUNT FOR HECTOR
AT DOG SCHOOL
AND . . .

- ☐ A-ARF
- ☐ Artist's model
- ☐ Banana peel
- ☐ Building plans
- ☐ Cat
- ☐ Chalk
- ☐ Clipboard
- ☐ Cloud
- ☐ Comic book
- ☐ Cook
- ☐ Cork
- ☐ Crown
- ☐ 2 Dancing dogs
- ☐ Doggy bag
- ☐ Doggy bank
- ☐ Dogwood
- ☐ Dunce cap
- ☐ Eraser
- ☐ Fire hydrant
- ☐ Flying bone
- ☐ 2 Forks
- ☐ Frankendog
- ☐ Genie
- ☐ Graduate
- ☐ Hammer
- ☐ Handkerchief
- ☐ "Hi, Mom!"
- ☐ "History Of
  Bones"
- ☐ Hockey stick
- ☐ "How To Bark"
- ☐ Leash
- ☐ Mail carrier
- ☐ Mush
- ☐ 2 Pencils
- ☐ P.T.A.
- ☐ Roller skates
- ☐ Saw
- ☐ 2 School bags
- ☐ Scooter
- ☐ Sun
- ☐ Sunglasses
- ☐ Triangle
- ☐ T-square

HUNT FOR HECTOR
AMONG THE DOG
CATCHERS
AND . . .

- [ ] Airplane
- [ ] Alien
- [ ] "Arf"
- [ ] Balloon
- [ ] Barber pole
- [ ] Carrots
- [ ] 5 Cats
- [ ] 3 Chimneys
- [ ] 3 Dog bowls
- [ ] 7 Dog catchers
- [ ] Doghouse
- [ ] Drums
- [ ] Firedogs
- [ ] 4 Fire hydrants
- [ ] Fisherdog
- [ ] 2 Flagpoles
- [ ] Flying saucer
- [ ] Gas mask
- [ ] 2 Howling dogs
- [ ] "Keep Things Clean"
- [ ] Mailbox
- [ ] Manhole cover
- [ ] 9 Police dogs
- [ ] 2 Restaurants
- [ ] Roadblock
- [ ] Rock and roll dog
- [ ] Santa dog
- [ ] Scout
- [ ] Shower
- [ ] Slice of pizza
- [ ] Streetlight
- [ ] 4 Super hero dogs
- [ ] Telephone
- [ ] Trail of money
- [ ] Trash can
- [ ] Tree
- [ ] 10 Trucks
- [ ] Turtle
- [ ] TV antenna
- [ ] TV camera
- [ ] Umbrella

HUNT FOR HECTOR WHERE THE RICH AND FAMOUS DOGS LIVE AND . . .

- ☐ Admiral
- ☐ Alligator
- ☐ Artist
- ☐ Bank
- ☐ "Big Wheel"
- ☐ Bird bath
- ☐ Blimp
- ☐ Bone chimney
- ☐ Candle
- ☐ Castle
- ☐ Cat
- ☐ 2 Cooks
- ☐ Crown
- ☐ Dog fish
- ☐ Dog flag
- ☐ Dog prince statue
- ☐ 2 Dog-shaped bushes
- ☐ Door dog
- ☐ Fat dog
- ☐ Fire hydrant
- ☐ Fisherdog's catch
- ☐ 2 Golfers
- ☐ Guard
- ☐ Heart
- ☐ Heron
- ☐ High rise condos
- ☐ Human
- ☐ 3 Joggers
- ☐ 6 Limousines
- ☐ Periscope
- ☐ Pillow
- ☐ Pool
- ☐ Sipping a soda
- ☐ Star
- ☐ Tennis player
- ☐ TV antenna
- ☐ Umbrella
- ☐ Violinist
- ☐ Water-skier
- ☐ Whale

HUNT FOR HECTOR AT THE K-9 CLEANUP AND ...

HUNT FOR HECTOR
AT THE SUPER
DOG BOWL
AND . . .

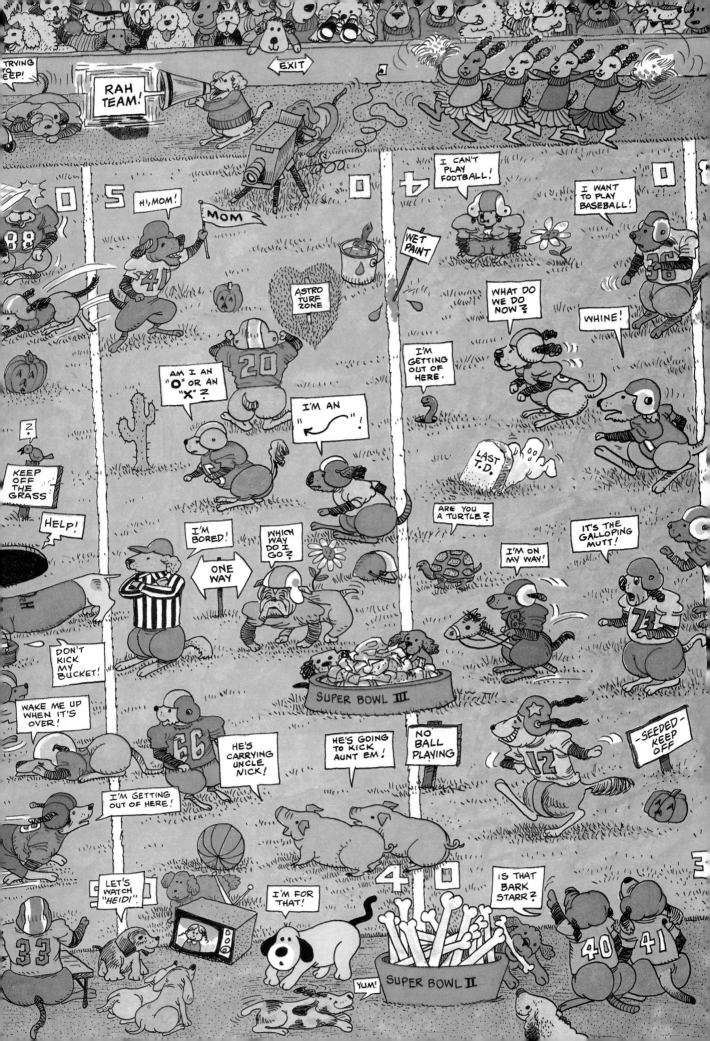

HUNT FOR HECTOR
AT THE DOG MALL
AND . . .

- ☐ Ball
- ☐ Balloon
- ☐ Barber shop
- ☐ Bat
- ☐ Bird's house
- ☐ Candle
- ☐ Candy cane
- ☐ 2 Cats
- ☐ Cheerleader
- ☐ Clown
- ☐ 2 Cookies
- ☐ Cup
- ☐ Dog bowls "Sale"
- ☐ Dog cake
- ☐ Doghouse
- ☐ Fish
- ☐ Flamingo
- ☐ Ghost
- ☐ Headphones
- ☐ Heart
- ☐ Helmet
- ☐ Howling Dog
- ☐ Human
- ☐ Ice cream cone
- ☐ Knight in armor
- ☐ Lollipop
- ☐ Mask
- ☐ Mouse
- ☐ Newsdog
- ☐ Newspaper reader
- ☐ Nut
- ☐ Paper airplane
- ☐ Pelican
- ☐ Pizza slice
- ☐ Police dog
- ☐ Pumpkin
- ☐ Scarf
- ☐ Stool
- ☐ Sunglasses
- ☐ Tennis racket
- ☐ Tire
- ☐ 2 Trash baskets
- ☐ Trophy
- ☐ Waiter

HUNT FOR HECTOR AT THE DOG OLYMPICS AND . . .

HUNT FOR HECTOR
AT THE TV QUIZ
SHOW
AND . . .

- ☐ "Answer"
- ☐ Ape
- ☐ Astronaut
- ☐ Band
- ☐ Binoculars
- ☐ 2 Birds
- ☐ Candle
- ☐ Cap
- ☐ Cue cards
- ☐ Director
- ☐ Elephant
- ☐ Fairy dog
- ☐ Fire hydrant
- ☐ Flashlight
- ☐ Flowerpot
- ☐ Giant dog bowl
- ☐ Giraffe
- ☐ Gold bar
- ☐ Hot dogs
- ☐ "Howl"
- ☐ "Junk Food"
- ☐ King dog
- ☐ Leash
- ☐ "Let's Go Dogs"
- ☐ Lunch box
- ☐ 4 Microphones
- ☐ Mouse
- ☐ Oil can
- ☐ Party hat
- ☐ Pearls
- ☐ Photographer
- ☐ "Quiet"
- ☐ Ring
- ☐ Robot
- ☐ Sleeping dog
- ☐ Snowman
- ☐ Sock
- ☐ Steak
- ☐ Straw hat
- ☐ "Take 1"
- ☐ 5 TV cameras
- ☐ TV set
- ☐ "V.I.P. Room"

HUNT FOR HECTOR
IN SPACE AND ...

- ☐ Bark Vader
- ☐ Boat
- ☐ Boney Way
- ☐ Book
- ☐ Bow-wow land
- ☐ Boxing glove
- ☐ Cat
- ☐ Condo
- ☐ Dog catcher
- ☐ Dog graduate
- ☐ Dog trek
- ☐ Doggy bag
- ☐ Duck Rogers
- ☐ Emergency stop
- ☐ Fire hydrant
- ☐ Flying
  dog house
- ☐ Flying food dish
- ☐ Jail
- ☐ Kite
- ☐ Launch site
- ☐ Lost and found
- ☐ Mail carrier
- ☐ Map
- ☐ Moon dog
- ☐ "No Barking"
- ☐ Parachute
- ☐ Pirate
- ☐ Pizza
- ☐ Planet of
  the bones
- ☐ Planet of
  the dogs
- ☐ Police dog
- ☐ Pup tent
- ☐ Puppy trainer
- ☐ Robot dog
- ☐ Sleeping dog
- ☐ Space circus
- ☐ Surfboard
- ☐ Swimming pool
- ☐ Tire
- ☐ Unicycle
- ☐ Vampire dog
- ☐ Vanishing dog

HUNT FOR HECTOR IN DOGTOWN AND . . .

- ☐ "The Arf Building"
- ☐ Barbecue
- ☐ Bird bath
- ☐ Boat
- ☐ Bone crop
- ☐ Bookstore
- ☐ 2 Broken clocks
- ☐ 8 Broken windows
- ☐ 2 Cats
- ☐ "Curb Your Human"
- ☐ Dance studio
- ☐ 5 Fire hydrants
- ☐ Flag
- ☐ "For Rent"
- ☐ Fountain
- ☐ "Frozen Dog Food"
- ☐ Gas station
- ☐ "Happy Dog Mush"
- ☐ 3 Hard hats
- ☐ Ice cream truck
- ☐ Jogger
- ☐ Lawn mower
- ☐ Mail carrier
- ☐ Mechanic
- ☐ Motorcycle
- ☐ Movie theater
- ☐ Newsdog
- ☐ "People Catcher"
- ☐ Piano
- ☐ Pool
- ☐ Santa Claus
- ☐ Sleigh
- ☐ Sock
- ☐ Video shop
- ☐ Wagon
- ☐ Water tower
- ☐ Weather vane
- ☐ Window washer

HUNT FOR HECTOR   SEARCH FOR SAM   FIND FREDDIE   LOOK FOR LISA

LOOK FOR LISA

WHERE ARE THEY?

LOOK FOR LISA AT THE MARATHON AND ...

- ☐ Alien
- ☐ Alligator
- ☐ Ape
- ☐ Astronaut
- ☐ 2 Banana peels
- ☐ Barbell
- ☐ 5 Bats
- ☐ Big nose
- ☐ Cable car
- ☐ Cake
- ☐ Caveman
- ☐ 8 Chimneys
- ☐ Clown
- ☐ Convict
- ☐ Deep sea diver
- ☐ Drummer
- ☐ 2 Elephants
- ☐ Fire fighter
- ☐ Fish
- ☐ Flying carpet
- ☐ Football player
- ☐ Frankenstein monster
- ☐ Horse
- ☐ Ice skater
- ☐ Long-haired lady
- ☐ Man in a barrel
- ☐ Moose head
- ☐ Octopus
- ☐ Pig
- ☐ 6 Quitters
- ☐ Santa Claus
- ☐ Skier
- ☐ Sleeping jogger
- ☐ Snow White
- ☐ Tuba
- ☐ 2 Turtles
- ☐ Vampire
- ☐ Viking
- ☐ Waiter
- ☐ Worm

LOOK FOR LISA
AFTER SCHOOL
AND . . .

- ☐ Airplane
- ☐ 2 Aliens
- ☐ Beanie
  with propeller
- ☐ Beard
- ☐ Blackboard
- ☐ Books on wheels
- ☐ Bucket
- ☐ Bus driver
- ☐ "Class brain"
- ☐ Clown
- ☐ Coach
- ☐ Dog
- ☐ Fire hydrant
- ☐ Football player
- ☐ Ghost
- ☐ Hockey player
- ☐ "Junior"
- ☐ Man trapped
  in a book
- ☐ 3 Mice
- ☐ Monkey
- ☐ Periscope
- ☐ Photographer
- ☐ Piano player
- ☐ Pillow
- ☐ "P.U."
- ☐ Pumpkin
- ☐ Radio
- ☐ Sailor
- ☐ School mascot
- ☐ Scooter
- ☐ Shopping cart
- ☐ Skateboard
- ☐ Ski jumper
- ☐ Socks
- ☐ Sports car
- ☐ Sunglasses
- ☐ Tepee
- ☐ Top hat
- ☐ Trash basket
- ☐ Unicorn
- ☐ Wagon

LOOK FOR LISA AT THE ROCK CONCERT AND . . .

- [ ] Alligator
- [ ] Apple
- [ ] Artist
- [ ] Beans
- [ ] Clown
- [ ] 2 Dogs
- [ ] Dwarf
- [ ] "Empty TV"
- [ ] Farmer
- [ ] Football player
- [ ] 4 Ghosts
- [ ] Giraffe
- [ ] 3 Guitars
- [ ] Heart
- [ ] 2 Hippos
- [ ] Hot dogs
- [ ] Hot foot
- [ ] Jogger
- [ ] Lamppost
- [ ] Lost balloon
- [ ] Magician
- [ ] "No Bus Stop"
- [ ] Pig
- [ ] Pink flamingo
- [ ] Pizza delivery
- [ ] Real cross wind
- [ ] Record albums
- [ ] Robot
- [ ] Rock
- [ ] Rock queen
- [ ] Roll
- [ ] Rooster
- [ ] Scarecrow
- [ ] School bus
- [ ] Skateboard
- [ ] 15 Speakers
- [ ] Stars
- [ ] Tent
- [ ] "Too Heavy Metal"
- [ ] Turtle
- [ ] Witch
- [ ] Zebra

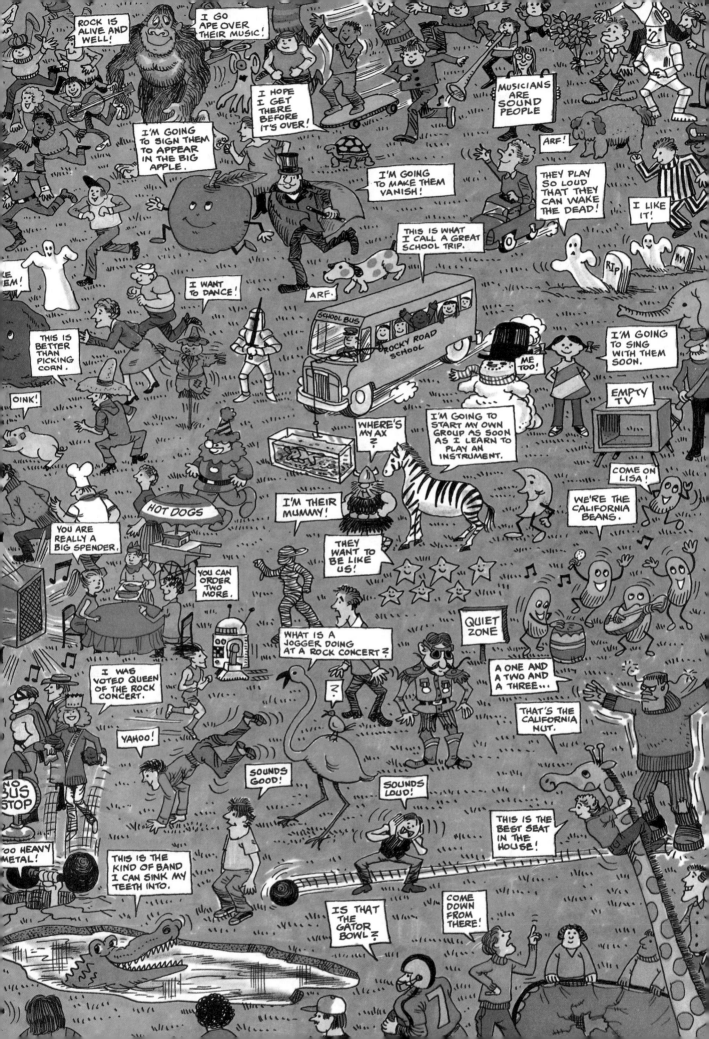

LOOK FOR LISA
ON THE FARM
AND . . .

- ☐ Ax
- ☐ Basketball hoop
- ☐ Birdbath
- ☐ Bubble gum
- ☐ 4 Chickens
- ☐ Covered wagon
- ☐ 2 Cows
- ☐ Dart board
- ☐ Deer
- ☐ 2 Ducks
- ☐ Flower bed
- ☐ Fox
- ☐ 3 Giant apples
- ☐ Giraffe
- ☐ Goat
- ☐ Haunted house
- ☐ Heart
- ☐ 3 Horses
- ☐ Igloo
- ☐ "Junk Food"
- ☐ 4 Kites
- ☐ Lion
- ☐ Milk containers
- ☐ 2 Monsters
- ☐ Mule
- ☐ Note in
      a bottle
- ☐ Piggy bank
- ☐ 2 Pigs
- ☐ Popcorn
- ☐ Rooster
- ☐ Satellite dish
- ☐ 5 Scarecrows
- ☐ Shark fin
- ☐ 2 Surfers
- ☐ Tractor
- ☐ Turkey
- ☐ Turtle
- ☐ TV antenna
- ☐ Used tire
- ☐ Well
- ☐ Worm

LOOK FOR LISA AT THE BEACH AND . . .

- ☐ Artist
- ☐ Barrel of pickles
- ☐ Birdbath
- ☐ Boot
- ☐ 3 Bottles with notes
- ☐ Bubble gum
- ☐ 4 Cactuses
- ☐ 2 Clowns
- ☐ Cow
- ☐ Crocodile
- ☐ Dart thrower
- ☐ 4 Flying fish
- ☐ Hammerhead shark
- ☐ Leaking boat
- ☐ Lifesaver
- ☐ Litterbug
- ☐ Lost bathing suit
- ☐ 3 Mermaids
- ☐ Motorcyclist
- ☐ Mummy
- ☐ Musician
- ☐ Oil rig
- ☐ Pirate ship
- ☐ Polluted area
- ☐ 3 Radios
- ☐ Robinson Crusoe
- ☐ Rowboat
- ☐ Sailfish
- ☐ Seahorse
- ☐ Sea serpent
- ☐ Sleeping man
- ☐ Skull cave
- ☐ Stingray
- ☐ Submarine
- ☐ 6 Surfboards
- ☐ Telescope
- ☐ Thief
- ☐ Tricyclist
- ☐ Very quick sand
- ☐ 2 Water skiers

LOOK FOR LISA AT THE BIG SALE AND . . .

- ☐ Bicycle built for two
- ☐ Book department
- ☐ Broken dish
- ☐ Carrot
- ☐ Cash register
- ☐ Chauffeur
- ☐ Earmuffs
- ☐ Elephant
- ☐ Fairy godmother
- ☐ Falling $
- ☐ 2 Fish
- ☐ Fishing pole
- ☐ Frying pan
- ☐ "1/2 off"
- ☐ Kite
- ☐ Ladder
- ☐ Man with sore feet
- ☐ Moose head
- ☐ Mouse
- ☐ Octopus
- ☐ Paint brush
- ☐ Paper plane
- ☐ Perfume counter
- ☐ Pogo stick
- ☐ Pole-vaulter
- ☐ Robot
- ☐ Rocket ship
- ☐ Rope climber
- ☐ Santa Claus
- ☐ Skier
- ☐ 2 Sleeping shoppers
- ☐ "Stale"
- ☐ Strange mirror
- ☐ Super hero
- ☐ Tall person
- ☐ Telescope
- ☐ Toy department
- ☐ Up and down escalator
- ☐ Vampire

LOOK FOR LISA
AROUND THE
WORLD AND . . .

- [ ] Bear
- [ ] Big foot
- [ ] 2 Bridge builders
- [ ] Cactus
- [ ] Camel
- [ ] Cowboy
- [ ] Cup of coffee
- [ ] Cup of tea
- [ ] Dog
- [ ] Eskimo
- [ ] 12 Fish
- [ ] 2 Flying saucers
- [ ] Golfer
- [ ] Heart
- [ ] Ice castle
- [ ] Igloo
- [ ] Kangaroo
- [ ] Lighthouse
- [ ] Lion
- [ ] Mermaid
- [ ] Merman
- [ ] Oil well
- [ ] Ox
- [ ] 6 Penguins
- [ ] Rock singer
- [ ] 4 Sailboats
- [ ] Sea serpent
- [ ] 4 Skiers
- [ ] 2 Snowmen
- [ ] Stuck ship
- [ ] Submarine
- [ ] 3 Surfers
- [ ] Telescope
- [ ] 6 "Travel Agent" signs
- [ ] Tug boat
- [ ] T.V. set
- [ ] Unicorns in Utah
- [ ] Viking ship
- [ ] Walrus
- [ ] Whale

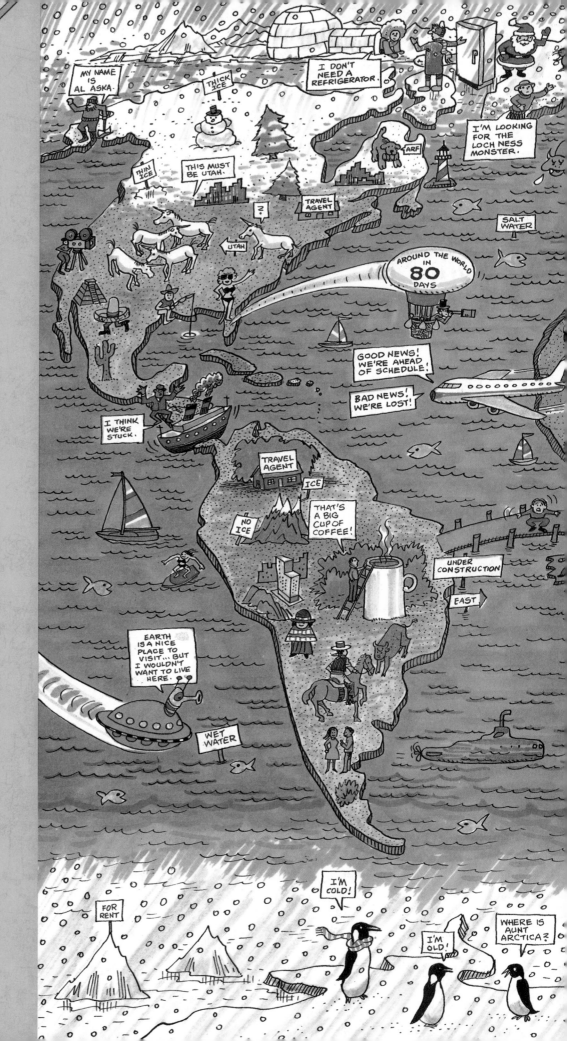

LOOK FOR LISA AT THE LIBRARY AND . . .

- ☐ Angel
- ☐ Banana peel
- ☐ Baseball cap
- ☐ Basketball players
- ☐ Book in a bottle
- ☐ 2 Bowling balls
- ☐ 4 Bullet holes
- ☐ Caveman
- ☐ Clown
- ☐ Copy machine
- ☐ 2 Cowboys
- ☐ Doctor
- ☐ Flying saucer
- ☐ Football
- ☐ Giant
- ☐ Hamburger
- ☐ Hammer
- ☐ Happy face
- ☐ 4 Hearts
- ☐ Hockey stick
- ☐ Horse
- ☐ Hula hoop
- ☐ Humpty Dumpty
- ☐ Moon
- ☐ Mummy and child
- ☐ Palm tree
- ☐ Paper plane
- ☐ 2 Parrots
- ☐ Pizza
- ☐ 7 "Quiet" signs
- ☐ 2 Radios
- ☐ Red wagon
- ☐ Referee
- ☐ Ship
- ☐ Skis
- ☐ 3 Skulls
- ☐ Telescope
- ☐ Tennis racket
- ☐ Tiny people
- ☐ TV camera
- ☐ Vacuum cleaner
- ☐ Worn tire

LOOK FOR LISA
AT THE
AMUSEMENT PARK
AND . . .

- ☐ Astronaut
- ☐ 15 Balloons
- ☐ Baseball
- ☐ Bomb
- ☐ Cactus
- ☐ Cheese
- ☐ Diplodocus
- ☐ "Do Not Read This"
- ☐ Entrance
- ☐ Exit
- ☐ Fishing hole
- ☐ 5 Ghosts
- ☐ Gorilla
- ☐ Graduate
- ☐ Headless man
- ☐ High diver
- ☐ Horse
- ☐ "Hot Dogs"
- ☐ "House Of Horrors"
- ☐ "Kisses"
- ☐ "Low Tide"
- ☐ 4 Mice
- ☐ 3 Monsters
- ☐ Mummy
- ☐ "No U-Turns"
- ☐ Pear
- ☐ Rocket
- ☐ Santa Claus
- ☐ "Scrambled Eggs"
- ☐ Skateboard
- ☐ Skull
- ☐ Snowman
- ☐ Thirteen o'clock
- ☐ Trash can
- ☐ Umbrella
- ☐ Vampire
- ☐ Witch

LOOK FOR LISA AT THE FLEA MARKET AND . . .

- ☐ Ape
- ☐ Bag of peanuts
- ☐ Baseball cards
- ☐ Bathtub
- ☐ Bicycle
- ☐ 2 Bird cages
- ☐ Box of records
- ☐ 2 Cactuses
- ☐ Candle
- ☐ Clown doll
- ☐ Cowboy
- ☐ 2 Dogs
- ☐ Duck
- ☐ 3 Fish
- ☐ Flower
- ☐ Football
- ☐ 2 Frogs
- ☐ Garbage basket
- ☐ Gas mask
- ☐ Giant shoe
- ☐ Graduate
- ☐ Hammer
- ☐ Knight in armor
- ☐ Lamp shade
- ☐ Man in bottle
- ☐ 2 Men with fleas
- ☐ Monster hand
- ☐ Pearl necklace
- ☐ Piggy bank
- ☐ Potted palm plant
- ☐ Rocking chair
- ☐ Saddle
- ☐ Scoutmaster
- ☐ Smoke signals
- ☐ Spinning wheel
- ☐ Sunglasses
- ☐ Tennis racket
- ☐ Toy locomotive
- ☐ Trumpet
- ☐ Yo-yo

LOOK FOR LISA
AS THE CIRCUS
COMES TO TOWN
AND . . .

- ☐ Ape
- ☐ Baby carriage
- ☐ 6 Balloons
- ☐ 2 Batons
- ☐ Bird
- ☐ Cactus
- ☐ Camel
- ☐ Candle
- ☐ Cannon
- ☐ Cat
- ☐ 13 Clowns
- ☐ 8 Dogs
- ☐ 5 Elephants
- ☐ "Exit"
- ☐ "For Rent"
- ☐ Giraffe
- ☐ 5 Happy faces
- ☐ 2 Indians
- ☐ Jack-in-the-box
- ☐ 2 Keystone cops
- ☐ Lion
- ☐ 2 Martians
- ☐ "Not Wet Paint"
- ☐ Rabbit
- ☐ Super hero
- ☐ 7 Tents
- ☐ Ticket seller
- ☐ Tightrope walker
- ☐ Tin man
- ☐ Top hat
- ☐ Turtle
- ☐ 3 Umbrellas
- ☐ Unicycle
- ☐ Weightlifter
- ☐ Witch

LOOK FOR LISA   FIND FREDDIE   SEARCH FOR SAM   HUNT FOR HECTOR

SEARCH FOR SAM

WHERE ARE THEY?

SEARCH FOR SAM IN CAT CITY AND . . .

SEARCH FOR SAM
ON FRIDAY THE
13TH AND . . .

- [ ] Apple
- [ ] Ax
- [ ] Balloon
- [ ] 7 Bats
- [ ] 4 Black cats
- [ ] Bomb
- [ ] Candy cane
- [ ] Chicken
- [ ] Coffin
- [ ] Condos
- [ ] Cow
- [ ] Football
- [ ] "Ghost Office"
- [ ] 6 Ghosts
- [ ] Heart
- [ ] "Helping Hand"
- [ ] Junior vampire
- [ ] Kite eater
- [ ] Mad doctor
- [ ] Mailbox
- [ ] Man's head
- [ ] Mirror
- [ ] Mouse
- [ ] "No Screaming"
- [ ] Paint bucket
- [ ] Pirate
- [ ] 13 Pumpkins
- [ ] Quicksand
- [ ] Rabbit
- [ ] Ship
- [ ] Shovel
- [ ] Skull
- [ ] Snake
- [ ] 13 "13s"
- [ ] Trunk
- [ ] Turtle
- [ ] TV set
- [ ] Two-headed
  monster
- [ ] Vampire

SEARCH FOR SAM
AT THE FAT CAT
HEALTH CLUB
AND . . .

- ☐ Bird
- ☐ Bird cage
- ☐ Bone
- ☐ Bowling ball
- ☐ Broken chair
- ☐ 2 Cactus
- ☐ Daydream
- ☐ Dog
- ☐ Drumstick
- ☐ Dumbbells
- ☐ Escaped convict
- ☐ "Fat
     Is Beautiful!?"
- ☐ Fattest cat
- ☐ 2 Fish
- ☐ 6 Fish bones
- ☐ Fish bowl
- ☐ 4 Gym bags
- ☐ 3 Hearts
- ☐ 2 Ice cream
     cones
- ☐ Instructor
- ☐ Jump rope
- ☐ "Lose It!"
- ☐ 3 Mice
- ☐ 2 Milk
     containers
- ☐ Paper bag
- ☐ Pizza
- ☐ Quitter
- ☐ Roller skates
- ☐ Scratching post
- ☐ Sleeping cat
- ☐ Sore feet
- ☐ "Steam Room"
- ☐ 2 Stools
- ☐ Sunglasses
- ☐ Talking scale
- ☐ "Think Thin"
- ☐ Torn pants
- ☐ 4 Towels
- ☐ Wallet
- ☐ Woman

SEARCH FOR SAM AT THE MIDNIGHT MEOWING AND . . .

- ☐ Alarm clock
- ☐ 3 "Arf"
- ☐ 2 Birds
- ☐ Broken window
- ☐ 3 Brooms
- ☐ 7 Cannonballs
- ☐ "Cat Power!"
- ☐ Dog
- ☐ 2 Dog bones
- ☐ Dog dish
- ☐ Doll
- ☐ Egg
- ☐ 2 Fish bones
- ☐ Floor mat
- ☐ 3 Flower pots
- ☐ Ghost
- ☐ Hockey stick
- ☐ "Hush"
- ☐ "I like it!"
- ☐ Loudest screamer
- ☐ Microphone
- ☐ Mouse
- ☐ "No Meowing Zone"
- ☐ Open gate
- ☐ Phonograph
- ☐ Piggy bank
- ☐ Pillow
- ☐ Pumpkin
- ☐ Rhino
- ☐ Shoe
- ☐ Sleeping cat
- ☐ Slice of pizza
- ☐ Spaceship
- ☐ Stool
- ☐ Tin can
- ☐ Tire
- ☐ 4 Trash cans
- ☐ Witch
- ☐ Yo-yo

SEARCH FOR SAM AT THE DISCO AND . . .

SEARCH FOR SAM
AT THE BATTLE
OF CATS AND
MICE AND . . .

SEARCH FOR SAM
IN ANCIENT EGYPT
AND . . .

SEARCH FOR SAM
AT THE CAT SHOW
AND . . .

- ☐ Banjo
- ☐ Beach chair
- ☐ Bird
- ☐ Black cat
- ☐ Cat costume
- ☐ Cat guard
- ☐ Cat in a hat
- ☐ Cat on a woman's head
- ☐ Clown
- ☐ Cow
- ☐ Curtain
- ☐ 2 Dogs
- ☐ Elephant
- ☐ Fat cat
- ☐ 2 Fish bowls
- ☐ Fishing pole
- ☐ Groucho cat
- ☐ Hobo cat
- ☐ Jogging cat
- ☐ 3 Judges
- ☐ Light bulb
- ☐ Lion
- ☐ "Moo Juice"
- ☐ Mouse
- ☐ Photographer
- ☐ Pizza
- ☐ Pool
- ☐ "Princess"
- ☐ Scaredy cat
- ☐ Scarf
- ☐ Scratching post
- ☐ Sombrero
- ☐ Sunglasses
- ☐ Telescope
- ☐ "The Real 1st Prize"
- ☐ Tombstone
- ☐ Trombone
- ☐ "Wanted" poster
- ☐ Witch

SEARCH FOR SAM
WITH THE
DOGBUSTERS
AND . . .

- ☐ "Bark 1-642"
- ☐ "Baseball
  Cards"
- ☐ Binoculars
- ☐ Bird
- ☐ Boat
- ☐ "Brooklyn"
- ☐ Blimp
- ☐ Bomb
- ☐ Cage
- ☐ Clown
- ☐ Crash
- ☐ Crocodile
- ☐ Dog house
- ☐ Fire hydrant
- ☐ Fish tank
- ☐ Happy face
- ☐ Helicopter
- ☐ "Hideout
  For Rent"
- ☐ Hockey stick
- ☐ Horse
- ☐ Manhole
- ☐ Monster
- ☐ 2 Mice
- ☐ Net
- ☐ Periscope
- ☐ "Pizza"
- ☐ "Poison Ivy"
- ☐ Pumpkin
- ☐ "Quiet"
- ☐ Rabbit
- ☐ Robot
- ☐ Rope ladder
- ☐ Saddle
- ☐ Super hero
- ☐ Surfer
- ☐ Tank
- ☐ Taxi
- ☐ Tent
- ☐ Truck
- ☐ Used tire
- ☐ Witch

SEARCH FOR SAM
AT THE NORTH
POLE AND . . .

SEARCH FOR SAM

FIND FREDDIE

HUNT FOR HECTOR

LOOK FOR LISA